IMAGES
of England

TRURO

THE SECOND SELECTION

CATHEDRAL LANE, *c.* 1960 Shoppers saunter through a breezy Cathedral Lane on a sunny day.

IMAGES
of England

TRURO
THE SECOND SELECTION

Compiled by
Christine Parnell

TEMPUS

First published 1999
Copyright © Christine Parnell, 1999

Tempus Publishing Limited
The Mill, Brimscombe Port,
Stroud, Gloucestershire, GL5 2QG

ISBN 0 7524 1643 X

Typesetting and origination by
Tempus Publishing Limited
Printed in Great Britain by
Midway Clark Printing, Wiltshire

Dedication
To my father, Byryn Woodward Mitchell RSS (1922-1999).

FATHER AND DAUGHTER. The author, aged nineteen months, holding hands with her father outside the blacksmiths' shop in Kenwyn Street in 1949.

Contents

Acknowledgements

I would like to express my sincere thanks to all those who have lent me photographs and given me information to help compile this book, including: Patricia and John Allam, Joan Andrews, Jean Bastian, Mrs C.B. Bennetts, Rovena Brown, Geoff and Pat Carveth, John Colston, Reg Colston, John Crowther, Phil Davey, Pat Davies, Les Douch, Jo Elsome-Jones, Jean Ferris, John Haswell, Renfred Knowles, Russell Martin, David and Betty May, Fred Mitchell, Margaret Mitchell, Michael and Jacqui Nancarrow, Bill Pankhurst, A.H. Pearne, Christine Penhaligon, Harry Pryce, Sybil Rapsey, W.J. Roberts, Barbara Rowe, Judy Rowe, Catherine Smerdon, Morwenna Southgate, Mervyn Steeds, Michael and Janet Stoot, Trevor Tallack, Barbara Thomas, Linda Thomas, Liz Trudgen, Mary Truran and Wilf and Gloria Tyack. I have made an effort to mention eveyone who has contributed. If I have inadvertantly overlooked anybody, please accept my deepest apologies.

Special thanks to my husband Peter for all his help and support and to my son David for his invaluable research.

BOSCAWEN STREET, *c.* 1950 Pearson's, the opticians and jewellers and the Gas Showrooms were later pulled down to enable both Littlewoods and the Midland Bank to expand. Today the opeway leading from Boscawen Street to High Cross is still known as Pearson's Ope.

Introduction

When I was collecting photographs for the first book in this series on Truro, many local people were convinced that they had nothing that would be interesting enough to incorporate into a book. When it was published I was suddenly inundated with offers of photographs from these same people who had realised that they did have something to offer after all. They had read *Truro*, enjoyed it and knew that photographs of the most ordinary things of days gone by could be very interesting after all, especially when the buildings had changed, almost beyond recognition, the faces and the fashions were gone and the way of life for most people today is so very different from that portrayed in the old photographs.

Yet again I have met many generous people who have spent time sorting out photographs and artifacts that they thought would be of use to me. Some people have just packed up their treasured photos and posted them to me without even thinking twice about their safety and I am very grateful to them.

Truro is a beautiful city, perhaps now more so than in the past. It is easy to forget that Middle Row must have made what is now a wide and elegant Boscawen Street into two narrow streets and that ingots of tin lying in the road outside the old coinage hall could have caused a hazard. The various smelting works round the town would have poured smoke and dirt into the atmosphere and with the horse-drawn traffic the streets would have been less than perfect.

Nevertheless some of the beautiful features from those days remain. Certainly the Old Mansion House and Dolphin House are portrayed here. With our mixture of twisting, narrow streets surrounding wide Boscawen Street with its solid municipal building and with the cathedral rising gracefully from the heart of the city, Truro is shown as a lovely place of character and contrast.

Once again I have thoroughly enjoyed compiling a book about Truro. I hope it gives as much pleasure to those who read it.

Christine Parnell
Truro, June 1999.

BACK QUAY, *c.* 1900. The circus comes to town and children throng the quay to see the elephants and camels. Lemon Bridge can be seen on the left of the picture and the Market Inn on the right is noticeably different architecturally from what we see today.

One
Around the Town

Just like most towns, Truro has undergone many changes over the years, particularly in the last couple of decades, when shops seem to come and go almost overnight. In this chapter we take a walk round the city to view many of the sights and sites of the past.

QUAY STREET, *c.* 1960. On the left of the picture is the Palace Theatre and on the right is the Old Mansion House, built around 1700 for the Enys family. The Penfold pillar box beside the telephone kiosk is the type made from 1866 to 1879 and is still in use today.

DOLPHIN HOUSE, c. 1960. At the time of this photograph Dolphin House was used as a café known as The Dolphin Buttery. It has since been demolished to make Green Street a wider thoroughfare. Richard Lander, whose family crest was the dolphin, was born here when was known as The Fighting Cocks Inn. Richard (1804-1834) and his brother John (1807-1839) traced the source of the River Niger in Africa.

PACK UP YOUR TROUBLES. Military activities outside Dolphin House in Quay Street during The First World War show kitbags being loaded onto a horse-drawn wagon.

PEARSON'S, *c.* 1955 This is the building that was demolished in 1961 to make way for an extended Midland Bank. The Gas Showrooms next door have the latest range of equipment on display in their window.

A RARE VIEW IN 1961. This view of the cathedral was snapped by Mr Renfred Knowles, then manager of Scott Brown, gentlemen's outfitters. Pearson's has moved to new premises at the bottom of Lemon Street.

LOWER LEMON STREET, c. 1960. This is where many people would go to find a special present. Netherton and Worth sold beautiful gifts, and flowers and chocolates were available next door at Edwards'.

LONDON HOUSE. The building at the corner of Lower Lemon Street and Boscawen Street is pictured just before its transformation into the modern building of today. After the rebuilding it remained W.H. Smith but with was a much lighter and airier shop.

RIVER ALLEN, 1956. Today, instead of this second-hand car shop there is an attractive riverside walk with a footbridge leading from the shoppers' car park on the right to St Mary's Mews off to the left.

PASSMORE EDWARDS BUILDING. An unusual view of the public library and the boys' Technical School in Union Place, after the demolition of the Silvanus Trevail post office and before the Marks and Spencer store was built.

BOSCAWEN STREET. Hawken and Sons, tailors, with the famous golden ram suspended over the shop front has now been taken over by W.J. Roberts and the original ope has been moved closer to Lloyds' Bank. The prices of items in the window of Kemp's suggest that this was photographed during the 1960s.

MEMORABILIA. This Kemp's paper bag, with blue writing on a red oval, looks so familiar even though the shop is long gone. Placed on the bag is a bottle opener from Tonkins of Truro.

ARCADE WINDOW DISPLAY, 1954. The windows of W.J. Roberts show hosiery of every description. Further inside one can see an arrangement of table linen. To reach the shop door one had to wander through the arcade where there was always plenty to tempt the shopper.

FIFTY YEARS AFTER THE EVENT. In 1904 shoppers at Roberts were alarmed when a cow on the way to market wandered into the store and created havoc. In 1954 the event was commemorated by this tableau in the shop.

NEW UNDERWEAR DEPARTMENT, 1952. W.J. Roberts open a new lingerie department and the picture shows young Bill Roberts (now the managing director) presenting flowers to Mrs Moon (secretary to the founder). Also shown are Margaret Mansell, Mrs Colson, Cecil Roberts and Mary Fillbrook.

NEW EXTENSION, 1957. Roberts' gained a new extension to their store in 1957 and celebrated the opening in style. Left to right: Mr John Crowther, Mr Cornelius, Miss Hilton (fashion manageress), Dawn (head of modelling school), the mayor and mayoress – Councillor and Mrs Behenna, Mr Cecil Roberts and Mr John Webb (store manager).

CRIDDLE AND SMITH, late 1950s. A chair is suspended over the Criddle and Smith store in St Nicholas Street. For many years this local company was the place where choice furniture could be obtained.

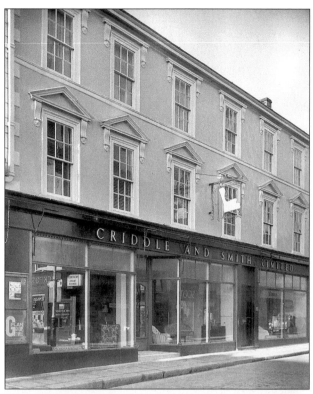

IT PAYS TO ADVERTISE. This enamelled tin advertisement once graced the wall of a local building and has been rescued for posterity by a Truro collector.

LUNCHTIME, *c.*1900. Horses concentrate on their nosebags outside the west front of the cathedral. They stand on cobbles which some may remember were covered over for a royal visit during the 1960s.

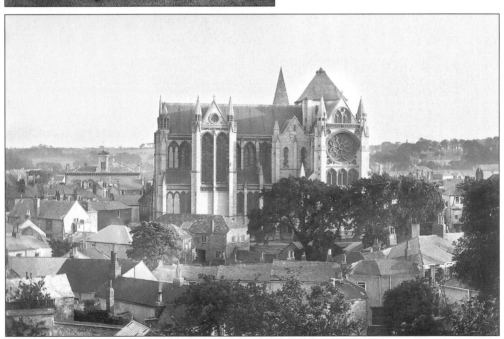

LOOK! NO TOWERS, *c.* 1890. This early photograph of the cathedral shows the copper tower beside the cap placed over the main tower-to-be. The west doors and the main aisle have still to be built. The municipal building in Boscawen Street can be seen on the left.

HIGH CROSS, *c.* 1899 A lone
gentleman strolls across the granite
setts of High Cross, probably on a
Sunday since the collection of taxis,
usually seen in old views at this point,
is absent.

THE WEST DOOR OF
THE CATHEDRAL,
c. 1950 Taken from a
rooftop in High Cross,
this view shows not only
the splendid carvings
round the west door of
the cathedral but also
Webb's Bargain Store in
St Mary's Street, the
draughtiest street in
Truro.

JORDAN'S BEFORE THE SECOND WORLD WAR. Smartly hatted ladies stop to read the newsboards outside Jordan's in Boscawen Street. The display of postcards in this shop doorway would represent a valuable find were they available for a modern collector today!

AN IRONMONGER'S WINDOW DISPLAY, *c.* 1920. Henley Bastian (Dick) wearing a suit and cap stands outside Bullen Brothers at 32/33, Boscawen Street. Later the store became Bullen and Scott and moved to Lower Lemon Street. Llewellyn Bailey is also in the photograph.

N. GILL AND SON. A large queue is attracted at the reopening of the store on 5 August (year uncertain). Next door is the civic restaurant, still a restaurant today and under the auspices of the Hall For Cornwall.

GILL'S ADVERTISEMENT. White lettering on a dark green background was the trade mark of Gill's sign. Such signs disappeared when Gill's were finally replaced by F.W. Woolworth.

CORNISH BANK, before 1922. The fountain, horse trough and street lamp were replaced by the war memorial in 1922. The fountain is now in Victoria Gardens. The pump is hidden by the children standing in front of it but it survives today and can be found in the cemetery in St Clements Hill.

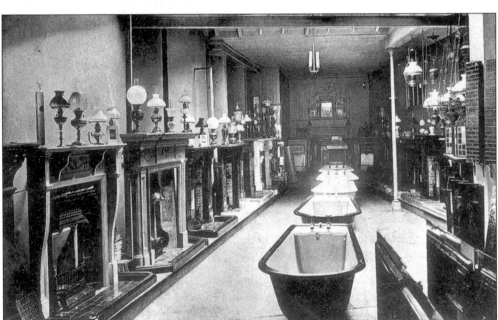

AN IRONMONGER'S SHOWROOM, c. 1910. Alfred Read's ironmongery was situated at 17 King Street and shows all the latest in fireplaces, lamps and baths. The store was certainly there by 1902 and survived until at least 1930 but its exact dates are not known.

THE RED LION HOTEL, early 1960s. The hotel basks in spring sunshine a few years before a tragic accident in 1967 when a runaway lorry crashed through the front. Built in 1761 as the Foote family house, it became an inn in 1769.

LAMPIER'S, 1950s. Under the proprietorship of Jack Lampier, the existing grocery shop was modernised and included a snack-bar and a frozen food department. The door in the centre leads to Elizabeth Colman, ladies' hairdresser.

THREE SPIRES. From the left can be seen St George's church, St George's chapel (now closed as a place of worship) and the cathedral.

PYDAR STREET, c. 1950. The rear of No. 91 Pydar Street is seen here in 1950. Unfortunately this historic old building has been demolished together with its variety of interesting windows.

FURNISS'S YARD, early 1940s. Mrs Joyce Andrew, holding her daughter, Gloria, stands below the steps in Furniss's Yard during the last war. Photographs of the Furniss Biscuit factory are hard to come by but many Truronians will remember the smell of gingerbreads, humbugs and peppermint rock that emanated from it with nostalgia.

ST MARY'S STREET, late 1950s. The little antique shop appears to cling to the building at the end of Squeeze-Guts Alley. Today it is a jeweller's shop and looks rather more substantial.

KENWYN STREET POST OFFICE.
Demolished in the name of progress, Kenwyn
Street post office now occupies a site in
Bosvigo Road but still glories in the name of
Kenwyn Street post office, to confuse the
unwary.

BOSVIGO ROAD, 1935. Granny Carveth
(Ellen) stands smiling outside her house in
Bosvigo Road, which is now the site of the
new Kenwyn Street post office.

THE LEATS, 1932. This is the area of The Leats behind the museum and close to the Health Office of today. The People's Palace was behind the wall on the left. When this photograph was taken not even bicycles were allowed in The Leats and kingfishers used to dart up and down between the bushes and the river.

THE LEATS, late 1960s. This is the same area of The Leats as shown in the previous photograph. On the left is the Health Office with the Register Office in front of it. The garden is gone now and the Register Office has moved to Dalvenie House next to the New County Hall.

HIGH CROSS, *c.* 1930. The staff of A. Tregaskiss, fruiterer and confectioner, stand outside the shop at 5 High Cross. The fruit is displayed in the lower part of the window with the sweets in their tall glass jars tastefully arrayed above. On the left is Mrs Flo Peartree with Mrs Doreen Wingham, before their respective marriages.

HARPIST FOR THE BARDS. Mrs Peggy Pollard, granddaughter of W.E. Gladstone and wife of Commander (Captain) Pollard is walking along Lower Lemon Street with Bill Haswell in about 1945. She regularly played the harp at gatherings of the Cornish Bards and Mr Haswell used to provide the transport for her (see p. 102).

JACK LAMPIER, *c.* 1920s. Jack Lampier strolls past the window of Pearson's, the opticians and jewellers, with Barclay's Bank in the background.

ALBERT RAPSEY IN BOSCAWEN STREET. On a rainy day Albert Rapsey makes his way along Boscawen Street, probably towards Jennings' in Victoria Square, where he worked for many years.

LONDON INN. The London Inn, pictured here during the late 1950s, was in Pydar Street. Like many other public houses in Truro it had been at various locations at different times and all those properties have since been demolished.

HIGHERTOWN INN, c. 1910. Richard Bray was the landlord of the Highertown Inn. It is still in business today, much extended and very popular for pub meals. It is now known as The County Arms. At the time this picture was taken the pub was in the middle of nowhere but today the town has grown up around it.

CALENICK STREET, *c*. 1950. The Golden Lion public house is no more. The site it once occupied, on the opposite side of the road to what is now the British Telecom offices, is a car park.

HOTEL CENTRAL, 1988. Yet another vanished Truro public house, the Hotel Central once faced onto Princes Square in the middle of Quay Street. Today the plot is vacant and serves as a temporary car park. There is talk of building flats on the site.

LANGDON'S CYCLE SHOP, 1952. Posing outside the door in New Bridge Street are Reg Langdon himself and a young Wilf Tyack.

THE JUNKET HOUSE, c. 1900. Children pose for the camera in the park alongside The Junket House (now known as Trennick Mill). The park was in its infancy and the small shrubs and saplings are now well grown making the park a haven for birds. Most people of Truro have fed the ducks there at some time.

TREGOLLS ROAD, *c.* 1955. Today this is a four-lane dual carriageway which has a central reservation bearing floral displays. All the cottages are gone from the right-hand side of the road as well as the garage and Tapper's fruit and vegetable wholesaler business. The last two buildings on the left are the old police station and the old Trafalgar Garage.

RIVERSIDE, *c.* 1960. The walk to the underpass of Morlaix Avenue can be seen on the left of the picture and colourful flowerbeds, carefully tended by Truro City Council, decorate the large area of grass. Today the Riverside Walk passes through this area and a rose bed, dedicated to the Burma Star Association is prominent.

READING ROOMS. In the 1930s when W.H. Smith and Son occupied London House at the corner of Lower Lemon Street and Boscawen Street there was a library and reading room upstairs which was open to the public.

WAR MEMORIAL. The memorial was unveiled on 15 October 1922 with much ceremony and a profusion of wreaths. No. 33 Boscawen Street in the background is the ironmonger's shop of Bullen Brothers.

THE RIVER, *c*. 1960. The ship *Rema* is moored at the rear of warehouses in Malpas Road, possibly delivering grain to Farm Industries Ltd. The crane across the water has apparently just unloaded coal from another vessel.

LEMON STREET, *c.* 1950. The dome of St John's church and Lander's Monument overlook a rainy Lemon Street. Thankfully nothing much has changed here except the design of the cars.

Two

Around the District

It is important to include people and scenes from around the district in a book about a city such as Truro. Their lives are inextricably bound up with the city dwellers. Wednesday is market day and the farmers have always come in to do business and congregate at the cattle market, which used to be on Castle Hill but is now way up on the Newquay Road. Many people come into town to do their shopping and once they reach the age of eleven the children are ferried in for their schooling. The villages round Truro are communities in their own right but Truro depends on them very much for its success and prosperity and they are very much a part of the city community.

ROYAL CORNWALL GAZETTE. What better way to reach the people of Cornwall than a local newspaper, established in 1801? People used to have to rely on the *Sherbourne Mercury* for their news, which was always somewhat out of date by the time it reached Cornwall and not particularly local in content.

TRESILLIAN BRIDGE, early 1900s. Youngsters pose for the camera on the bridge. The church and its hall are still there today but the children would be risking life and limb if they ventured into the road among today's traffic.

THE WHEEL INN. Although this picture was taken in the early part of the century, The Wheel Inn on the left has changed very little since that time. The buildings opposite, which include the Mens' Institute, were demolished for road widening.

THATCHED COTTAGE. Mr Roberts of Tresillian, outside the door of his home which adjoined the toll house. Both buildings have long since been pulled down.

ST NEWLYN EAST, *c.* 1914. The vicar and his family in the garden of the vicarage at St Newlyn East. Left to right, back row: Richard Gill, Archibald Eade, Percival Eade, Edward Eade. Front row: Jane Eade, Rokum Gill, Georgina Eade and baby daughter, Revd Isaac Broad Eade, Mary Jane Eade and granddaughter, Claudia Eade and Winifred Hilda Eade and her daughter, Hilda.

BLACKWATER, early 1900s. The camera always attracted an audience and even during haymaking everything stopped for a photograph.

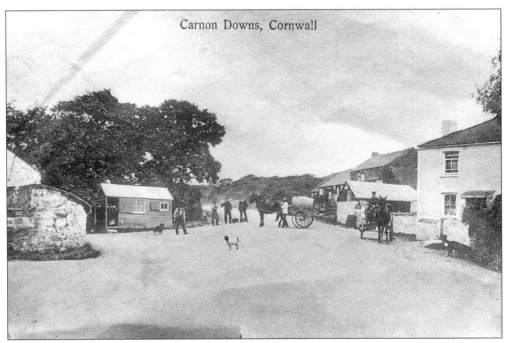

CARNON DOWNS, late nineteenth century. The building on the right is the kiddleywink and the road leading off to the left goes to Quenchwell. The water carrier is delivering to local inhabitants from his horse-drawn barrel.

CHACEWATER, EAST END, *c.* 1930. Apart from the shop ownership and the products on display little has changed over the years. However, it might not be so easy to cross the street today.

NORWAY INN. This public house was so named because ships from Norway used to come this far when the river was navigable. The Norwegian flag can be seen flying from the pole. The grassy area is now a car park and the building has been extended.

GLOWETH, *c*. 1950. The approach to the city is shown here before the introduction of the four-lane dual carriageway and large roundabout. The house on the right had to be demolished and the occupants re-housed in Threemilestone.

GLOWETH, *c*. 1950. A lone car travels towards Truro. The building shown is now part of the Treliske Hospital complex and no longer a leafy country retreat.

THE LOST CHURCH, *c.* 1930. St Piran's Oratory in the shifting sand dunes at Perranporth is protected by the structure shown in the photograph. It is the focal point of the St Piran's Day walk held on 5 March each year.

PERRANPORTH, *c.* 1930. The garage of S. Harvey-Mitchell separates Beach Road on the left from St Piran's Road on the right.

IDLESS, 1962. Smokey and his mistress, Mrs Olive Andrews, take some exercise on a cold February day. It looks as if Smokey has just had his mane brushed for the camera.

THE PANDORA INN, 1968. The beautiful Pandora Inn is popular with visitors and locals alike. Previously called The Ship it was renamed when ex-Royal Naval Captain Edwards took over as publican and named it after his ship. He had been sent to capture mutineers from Captain Bligh's *Bounty* but his ship was subsequently wrecked in the Pacific Ocean with much loss of life.

Three
All in a Day's Work

Just as with most aspects of life there have been great changes in the way people earn a living – if they are fortunate enough to have a job at all. There is no longer a smithy in Truro or any of the villages round about, no cattle drovers or even a solitary Johnny Onion with his bicycle and strings of onions. To keep abreast of technology people's jobs have changed dramatically but here we take a look at some of the occupations of Truronians in days gone by.

FILLING IN OF LEMON QUAY. During the 1920s work started on covering over the River Kenwyn between Lemon and Back Quays. Here outside the Municipal Building, probably in 1926, the men are hard at work with their concrete mixer creating the new car park; square yard by square yard.

THE NEW VIADUCT, *c.* 1900. Workmen take a break during the heavy labour of building pillars for the new viaduct which was to replace Brunel's wooden structure.

THE NEW 'VIADOCK'. Work has progressed on the new stone viaduct. Brunel's wooden one can be glimpsed through the right-hand arch. Also, on the right of the picture, is a group of bystanders, including a baby in an elegant carriage, watching the developments.

HARVEST TIME, *c*. 1880. A farmer and his three horses gather the harvest. The farm has not been identified but was close to Truro.

EXTRA HELP. Two ladies have arrived, perhaps to help or maybe they brought the croust or crib out to the field. This photograph gives a better view of the machinery. The farmer wears his tall hat and the ladies seem to be wearing clothing quite unsuitable for agricultural labour!

A SHOE FOR SMOKEY, *c.* 1960. Mr Hoare, the blacksmith/farrier at Shortlanesend, is busy shoeing Smokey, owned by Miss Joan Andrews. The tools of Mr Hoare's trade are neatly laid out in his box. When Mr Hoare retired Smokey was brought in to Truro to be shod by F.W. Mitchell and Son, the farriers in Kenwyn Street, who were the nearest to Idless.

SHORTLANESEND FORGE, *c.* 1960. Miss Andrews holds Smokey's head as the horse is attended to by the farrier outside his forge at Shortlanesend. The clutter beyond the horse is typical of forges of the time.

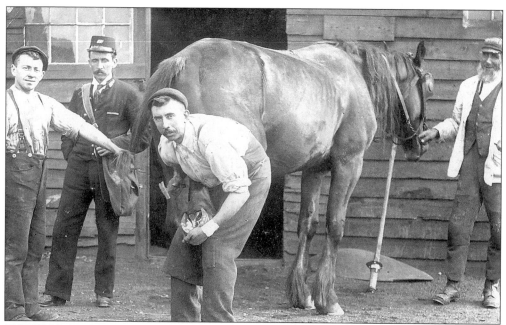

SHOEING AT BLACKWATER. Believed to have been taken at Blackwater at the turn of the century, this picture shows the local farrier hard at work and the postman standing by. The elderly gentleman at the horse's head has propped his hay dividers against the building.

FARMING AT IDLESS. Mr Howard Richards shows off his David Brown Cropmaster tractor, which is fitted with a Teagle broadcaster, on his farm at Idless in spring 1960.

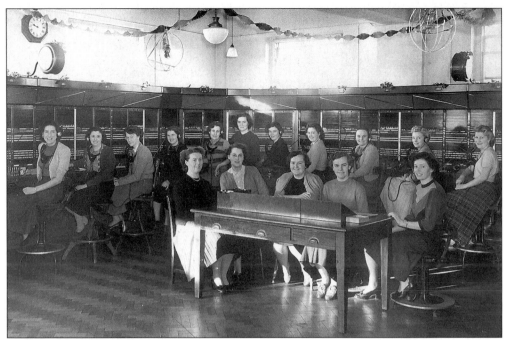

TELEPHONE ENQUIRY POINT. The ladies of the Truro Telephone Exchange are shown during the 1950s. Included are: Jon Haynes, Flo Pollard, Mary Ingram, Kitty Moyle, Douché Egerton, Heather Biddick, Ruby Martin, Lorraine Strobel, Yvonne Arnold, Sylvia Paul, Betty Capon, Vera Opie, Frances Hender and Betty Hodge.

NIGHT STAFF, *c.* 1950. The Truro Telephone Exchange is decorated for Christmas and the smiling staff include: Joe Bertolucci, Ernie Hill, Jackie Salmon, Ron Stanaway and Mr Biddick.

NUMBER PLEASE!, 1971. Jacqui Nancarrow, Cicily Stephens and Eileen Schmidt are busy working in the telephone exchange at Perran-ar-worthal.

A PAUSE IN THE PROCEEDINGS, c. 1950. Margaret Hill and Sheila Thomas take a break from operating their equipment at the telephone exchange to smile for the camera.

LAMPIER'S GROCERY STORES, 1920. This shop was situated at Nos 3 and 4 Boscawen Street. Here the staff have just taken delivery of a consignment of Vim, which is neatly stacked up on the pavement. The store's owner, Mr Thomas Arthur Lampier, is shown beside his wife Isabella. Also in the picture are Jack Lampier, Freddy Endean and Reggie Penhaligon.

ICE CREAM VENDOR, c. 1950. Mr G. Perry wheels his ice-crean trolley through Princes Street on a sunny day. There is little need to bother about interference from on-coming traffic.

CARVETH'S STATIONERS. Albert Trudgen stands in the doorway of Carveth's in Calenick Street in the early 1950s. He worked there for many years.

COMPETITION WINNERS, early 1950s. Jean Richards, Muriel Hill, Mary Rundle and Phyllis Webber were the winners of the County Cup for Fist Aid. They were members of the Truro Centre for the Red Cross and are pictured at Tolgullow House, Scorrier, the home of the Williams family.

AMOS JENNINGS, *c.* 1930. A Great Western Railway horse-drawn vehicle, loaded with Heinz Varieties stands outside the shop in Victoria Square. The gentlemen in the dark suits are Mr Amos Jennings and Mr Bill Jennings and the staff include Albert Rapsey, Frank Tremelling, Ron Solomon, A. Champion, B. Chasney, J. Whitford, B. Perry, B. Johns, J. Archer, J. Hendra, N. Turner, K. McLean and J. Crewes.

ARCHITECTS' DEPARTMENT, 1946. Members of the County Hall Architects' Department don their winter coats in January 1946. Included are: F. Mitchell, R. Harding, E.F. Tonkin, Mr Sifton, Mr Buckingham, Phil Chudley, Joe Murrish, Hilda Tamblyn, E.A. Love, Betty Skinner, Margaret Oatey, Nancy Rapson, Margaret Newman, ? Jones and H.G. Phillips.

HEAD GARDENER, *c.* 1930. Mr Henry Roberts, the head gardener at Malabar House, when it was a private residence, stops to fill his pipe. Malabar later became a home for the blind and an old folks' home and is currently being converted into luxury flats.

H.T.P. MOTORS STAFF PHOTOGRAPH, *c.* 1939. Jack Nancarrow is on the extreme left of the third row from the back but unfortunately there is no further information to identify the rest of the group.

SOLOMON AND METZ, PRINTERS, 1966. Hedley Bennetts and his father John Bennetts are seen here in their printing works in 1966. They are the grandson and son-in-law of the company's founder, Andrew Metz. The firm was founded in 1913 and continued until 1985.

PRINTING TRIO, 1966. Hedley Bennetts and his father are joined by Arthur Metz, the son of the founder of the firm Solomon and Metz in the printing works in Richmond Hill.

DAISY AT WORK, c. 1942. Nigel Ferris and his horse, Daisy (pulling a plough) stop to talk to young Harold Ferris at Porthgwidden Farm, Feock.

HOSE WORK AT COOSEBEAN, c. 1960. Walter Penfold and George Barnicoat (left) of the Cornwall County Fire Brigade train hoses towards Rotten Woods during an exercise in the early 1960s.

RIVER STREET, turn of the century. A gentleman studies Hicks's window in River Street. These premises extended right through to Kenwyn Street (see p. 100). The shipping office under Clyma's Temperance Hotel advertises tickets for the Canadian Pacific Railway and Steamship Lines.

REMOVAL MEN. Albert Colston (centre) stands outside Pickfords Depository in St Austell Street, late 1920s. For many years Pickfords had an office in King Street.

RETIREMENT CLOCK. Mr Harry Andrews is being presented with a clock on the occasion of his retirement as a Post Office Telephones Inspector. Mr Stephens is in the centre of the picture, which was taken at Trevint in Strangways Terrace. The clock worked beautifully for many years but when Mr Andrews died, in his nineties, the clock stopped and despite his daughter taking it for repair, it never worked properly again.

JOAN ANDREWS' RETIREMENT, 1983. Mr Harry Andrews is present at the retirement of his daughter, Miss Joan Andrews, when she, in turn, retired from British Telecom. Also shown in the picture is Reg Lomas.

MAN AT WORK, late 1960s. An elderly couple stop to chat with the workman in Boscawen Street attending to the 'Keep Left' bollards. W.H. Smith occupy a modernized London House and Martin's Bank is in the background.

Four

Time to Relax

After a hard day's work it is time to relax and the people of Truro engage in their favourite pastimes. Music has always been of great importance and here we see choirs, operatic societies, drama clubs and bands represented. There have always been plenty of sporting activities taking place and invariably the winners were photographed with their trophies. Here we have a selection showing Truronians at play.

LOOKING FOR TIDDLERS, June 1954. Angela Rapsey and Brian Hoskin have jam jars at the ready as they search for tiddlers in The Leats below Victoria Gardens.

ST MARY'S PARISH CHOIR, 1925. This choir was drawn from the parish of St Mary's and they would sing evensong in the cathedral when the cathedral choristers were on holiday. It was a popular choir and used to attract large congregations. Pictured at Lis Escop, Canon Lewis, his wife and daughter, are in the centre. Billy Trebell is behind Mrs Lewis, Fred Mitchell second from the left, front row and also included are: Ben Pearce, ? Newbury, Harold Whitburn, Percy Martin, Albert Lamerton, ? Lowry, ? Benallack, Fred Trewin, Arthur Pascoe, Judge Miners, George Holland, Ernie Colliver, Jack Lock, Gerald Stethridge, ? Richards, George Trebell, Ernie Holland, Charlie McLaughlin, Walter Warren, Harry Penhaligon, Harry Sampson, Spencer James, Abbey Trudgen, Monsy Bradley, Len Varker, Mr.A.P. Rowe, Mr Rich and Mr Philp.

TRURO CITY BAND, 1950s. Bandmaster, Mr Parker (centre left with bow tie) is shown with members of his band. Included are: Reg Stone, Allen Clift, Bill Clift, Sam Verran, Ivor Nicholls, L. Piper, A. Allen, F.Braund, R. Medlyn and W. Tremaine.

TRURO TOWN SILVER PRIZE BAND. This photograph, taken during the 1920s or 1930s shows the band proudly displaying an impressive array of trophies. The cup in the centre appears to be the same one which is displayed in the previous picture.

CATHEDRAL CHOIR, 1950. John Winter was an organist at The Cathedral at this time and is in the front row. In the back row, on the extreme right, is Richard Ratcliffe and third from the right is Michael Hicks. Also in the picture are Geoff Miller, Graham Carter, Guillaume Ormond.

PARADE OF CHORISTERS, 1906. The Diocesan Choral Union Festival was held in Truro in 1906 and the choristers are seen parading past the premises of the West of England Brush Company.

BOYS BRIGADE BAND, 1978. Members of the First Troop, Boys Brigade, St Georges Methodist church play in the waterfall gardens and the chapel, now closed for worship, can be seen behind them.

BOSVIGO SCHOOL CHOIR, 1968. The winners at the Music Festival at the Princess Pavillion in Falmouth proudly display their trophy. Amongst the group are: Judy Brannlund, Julie Whitford, Linda Williams, Lynne Wotton, Sarah Rowlands, Andrew Whitehouse, Timothy Feltham, Perran Gay, Sarah Norsworthy, Simon Whittall, Julie Tucker and Dorothy Dickinson. Holding the trophy is Lorraine Rowse.

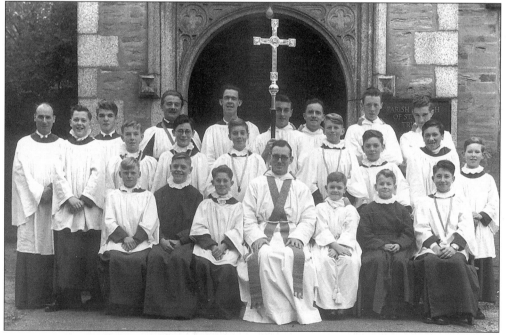

ST PAUL'S CHURCH CHOIR, c. 1957. Revd H. Miles-Brown sits in the centre of the front row. Choristers in the front row include Colin Hawke, Roger Lampier and Kenwyn Lampier. Behind are Nigel Tonkin, Charles Argall, Derek Hawke, Jimmy Pascoe, Peter Long, Barrie Perkins and Derry Drew.

SNOW WHITE. Members of Daniell Road School performed *Snow White* in 1952. Mary Stethridge is in the back row, second from left.

ORIENTAL LADIES. The only person who can be named in this picture is Gertrude Lock who is on the extreme right of the front row. The photograph was taken outside the Municipal Buildings in the 1930s.

AMATEUR DRAMATICS. In 1962 The Truro Amateur Operatic Dramatic Society gave a performance of *White Horse Inn*. The front group are: John Colston, Keith Rowe, Geoff Carveth and Cliff Sharpe.

CATHEDRAL SCHOOL PLAY. The cast of *The Tempest* take a curtain call after a performance in around 1953.

TRURO BAPTIST CHURCH. The congregation of the Baptist church are enjoying an afternoon out at Comprigney around the time of the First World War.

NATIVITY PLAY, 1951. Young people from Kenwyn church perform their annual nativity play. The cast includes: Bridget Peartree, Janet Stoot, Michael Stoot, Brian Barrett, Margaret Roberts, Jennifer Lanyon, Margaret Secretan, Kingsley Rowe, Ruth Hosken, Rosemary Kneebone, Jill Haynes, Mary Pearce, Marie Edyvean, Roger Flexman, Peter Rowe, Peter Rosevear, Diana Martin, Catherine Birch, Elizabeth Watkins, Peter Harper, Roger Farnworth, Doreen Nicholls and Wendy Fry.

BOYS BRIGADE, mid-1940s. This smiling group was on the way to summer camp in Somerset, a real treat during wartime. Left to right, back row: Michael Kneebone, Maurice Penrose, with Peter Hayes behind him, Clive Duke, Charlie Bray, Reg Colston, Capt. Davies and George Nancarrow. Front row: Brian Morton, Jimmy Penrose, Brian Hayes, Dennis Mitchell, John Pearn.

BROWNIES, c. 1960. The Third Truro, St Georges pack includes: Linda Westcott, Jennifer Gill, Ann Pedlar, Lydia Gallie and Madge Symons.

VISITING PACHYDERM. Jumbo (or is it Nellie?) the elephant takes a stroll along St Georges Road at the end of the nineteenth century. It appears that the keeper has detached the harness for a local photographer to record the scene while some local lads look on.

THE CIRCUS COMES TO TOWN, *c.* 1900. Before being allowed some freedom, Jumbo has lead the rest of the circus into town. Here they are seen having just come past Trafalgar post office at the bottom of Tregolls Road to start a parade through the city.

SUNDAY SCHOOL TREAT, 1914. Castle Street was a thriving community just before the Great War and this was probably to be their last Tea Treat before hostilities began. It was traditional for everyone to have a large saffron bun but judging by the size of the teapot shown in the left front of the picture it's unlikely that everyone got a cup of tea!

SNOW IN CASTLE HILL, 1947. Vera Gallie and Harry Westcott smile for the camera while Donald Gallie takes a break from clearing snow from the path.

YOUNG WIVES, *c.* 1955. The 'young wives' are seen having a celebration meal in the church hall of the old church at Highertown. The Revd Williams and his wife are shown in the centre at the back and Revd Michael Geach is on the left. Also included are Marion Bastian, Freddy Toy, Jack Thomas, Mrs Durston and Mr Tremayne.

CAMERA CLUB, late 1940s. Much credit goes to the members of this club for the survival of some of the photographs shown in this book. Among those standing are Harry Andrews, Ron Pedlar and Mr Dash; Joan Andrews is the only lady in the group.

SUNBEAMS AND GUARDS, *c.* 1943. The younger members of the Salvation Army were known as 'Sunbeams' and stand here in a row at the back. Among them are June Lee and her younger sister, who were evacuees. At the very back, Sybil Johns carries the flag. The guards with their round hats and lanyards include Bernice Groom, ? Ash, Barbara Savage, Rovena Davies, Ruth Davies, Kathleen Haynes, Rose ?, Pat Kellow, Loveday Sanders, ? Waller, Florence Blake, Dorothy Adams and Gwen Allen. The leader is Mrs Ridgers.

MR MEYRICK'S WALKERS, 1988. On 27 January 1988, the day of Truro's second flood of the year, Mr Meyrick led a team of walkers on a ramble and enjoyed a meal at the Trennick Mill. Later in the day the fire brigade was twice called out to pump out the cellars of Trennick Mill, which has always been prone to flooding and caught the full measure of this one. Pictured are: Mrs Norma Hocking, Mrs Olsen, John Bowden, Mac ?, Arthur Lyne, Mrs Edith Thompson, Mrs Hawke, Mr Meyrick, Dick Hale, Miss Jean Hunter, Mr Thompson, Olga Patterson, Barbara Rowe, Dick Patterson.

ST MARY'S CHAPEL, *c.* 1949. This is a gathering of the Methodist Youth Clubs at St Mary's chapel. Reg Colston is in the middle of the front row and also shown are Donald Gallie and his sister, Barry Pascoe, Charlie Bray and Brian and Peter Hayes.

BOTTLE FEEDING, *c.* 1948. Doris Haswell is seen feeding two piglets on whom she has taken pity. They had a cossetted upbringing beside the fireplace in her house in Pydar Street.

SELF PORTRAIT, 1964. Harry Andrews took this picture himself while pottering in his garage. He was a leading light in the Truro Camera Club.

TRURO BOWLING CLUB, *c.* 1969. A happy group of bowlers at Truro Bowling Green in Kenwyn Hill were snapped on a clear day. There are too many faces to name them all but included among them are: Howard and Ethel Batchelor, Jack and Lottie Fillbrook, Jack and Betty Parnell, John Knight, George Beard, Mel Ferris, Iris Pomery, Muriel Shute, Bert Eva and Mrs Robbins.

TRURO BOXING CLUB, c. 1935. Hardly a salubrious setting for a photograph, possibly taken in the vicinity of The People's Palace, but the fit young members of the boxing club look happy enough. The man in the centre is wearing a trophy belt. The man next to him in the cap is Hilmer 'Ben' Brannlund and the boy on the right in the front row is also called Hilmer Brannlund. Hilmer Brannlund came over from Sweden and married a Cornish girl. Later members of the family had a painting, decorating and sign writing business.

ST CLEMENTS FOOTBALL TEAM, 1952. The team played against Probus at Tregony and won the cup which is being received here by Brian Pascoe. Clive Duke is on the left and Vic Tozer is peeping over the head of the gentleman presenting the trophy. Behind the cup is Geoff Carveth and the others are Peter Richards, Roy Whitford, Geordie Simpson, Stewart Gilbert, Ken Gilbert and Michael Hill.

POST OFFICE XI, 1948/49. Back row from left: B. Martin, O. Gosling, D. Hutchings, H. Harfoot, Mr Gibbons (postmaster), R. Gummow, J. Richards, ? Lock, K. Gilbert, G. Ralph. Front row: H. Moore, B. Prowse, S.Venton, A.Rapsey, A.Thomas.

POST OFFICE XI, 1950. Mascot David Brannlund, wearing his Truro School uniform is kneeling in the front with Hilmer Brannlund behind him. The goalie is Russell Gummow and on his left is Jock Fenton with Jimmy Taylor in front.

GRAMMAR SCHOOL HOCKEY TEAM, 1955/56. The pupils of the former Truro County Grammar School for girls stand on the playing field, now Sainsbury's car park, overlooking the old County Hall. They are, left to right, back row: June Simmons, Anita Bertolucci, Ruth Butson, Mrs Joan Passmore, Angela Lavis, Cicily Warren, Angela Watt. Front row: Christine Collins, Yvonne Prisk, Rosemary Eva (with panda mascot and trophy), Joan Rule and Susan Opie.

CUP FINAL, 1934/35. The Devonshire and Cornwall Heavy Brigade R.A. before the Territorial Cup Final 1934/35. To the left of the rosette is Archie May.

CUP WINNERS, 1934/35. The victorious Devonshire and Cornwall XI pose again after the match with their trophy, joined by well-wishers and supporters.

WEST COUNTRY CHAMPIONS, 1951. Truro Girls' Secondary Modern School (Daniell Road) had such a marvellous netball team that the whole team was selected to play in the championship, rather than form a team picked from various schools. The victorious team is, left to right: Jean Curgenven, Angela Dexter, Sheila Teague, Mary Stethridge, Sylvia Trebell, Margaret Curnow, Barbara Solomon, Joan Grose and Barbara Kent.

ST PAUL'S SCHOOL, 1919. This St Paul's team beat Tywardreath by 2-1 to win the 1919 County Shield. Archie May is second from the left in the front row.

CHACEWATER CRICKET CLUB, 1939. The winners of the Loscombe League are shown here with their trophy and their mascot, David May. David's father, Archie, is third from the left on the back row.

CITY INN DARTS TEAM, 1956. An impressive array of trophies is on display and three members of the team have been identified. Reg Stone is top right, Jimmy Penrose is above the left darts board and J. Flynn is wearing the tartan tie.

THE GOOD SPORTS DARTS TEAM, late 1960s. Originally based at The Globe Inn in Frances Street, the team later moved to The Admiral Boscawen in Richmond Hill. In the photograph are, back row, left to right: Jack Coleman, Mike Miller, John Rowarth, Bill Hodge, Jack Thomas, Gerry Allen, Terry Hall, Doug Franklyn, Wally Annear, Barry Penfold, Bill Squires. Middle row: Dick Williams and George Champion. Front row: Jack Champion, Charlie Cowling, Des Solomon (landlord), Len Hoskins and Geoff Carveth.

TRURO ARGYLE AFC, 1913/14. Old Truronians will remember this football team but time has clouded memories and the author is unable to put any names to faces except the little chap sitting on the ball who was apparently known as 'Teddy'.

COUNTY OFFICERS XI, 1970s. All these men worked at the County Hall in Truro and played in both league and friendly games. Left to right, back row: Seymour, Pascoe, Knight, Carveth, Nightingale, Holloway. Front row: Hunt, Tammo, Hull, Hocking, Drew, Jewell.

Five

Events

Grouped together under this heading are some photographs which represent special milestones in people's lives and mark memorable occasions. They include wartime pictures, victory celebrations, Coronations and even events such as heavy snowfalls and floods.

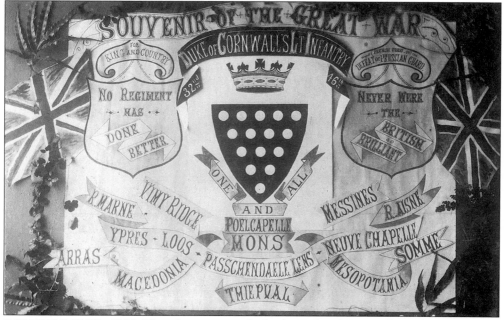

DCLI SOUVENIR, 1918. This plaque was made for the Duke of Cornwall's Light Infantry and lists the battles and campaigns in which the regiment had taken part up to that time.

THE FIRST WORLD WAR. This postcard was produced in France at the time of the Battle of Mons. Truro's Albert Colston is standing under the gun.

VICTORY CELEBRATION. Children of Truro don fancy dress at the end of the Second World War. Albert 'Abbey' Trudgen is standing in the back row.

84

PLAYING PLACE HOME GUARD. Back row, left to right: ? Stevens, Arthur Peters, ? Waller, ? Deacon, Lew Caple, John Lavin, ? Phillips, Reg Trebilcock, Reg Davey. Middle row: Arthur Watts, Hedley Martin, -?-, Edgar Ham, -?-, -?-, -?-, -?-, -?-, Jack James, Frank Davey. On chairs: ? Smith, -?-, ? Letcher, Col. Carey Morgan, Bill Rowe, ? Gallihawke, ? Drewett. On ground: ? Lampshire, Jim Tregunna, -?-, ? Williams, ? Clifford Radmore, Billy May, -?-, -?-, ? Caple, -?-. The photograph was taken outside the Home Guard hut which these days is a snooker club.

FARLEY FIELD, 1945. A victory celebration for the little ones in Farley's Field. In the photograph somewhere are Paul and Sheila Edmonds, Anne Braund, Joan and Fowey Cole, Christine Collins, Wendy and Pamela Grigg and Armorel Collett.

ICELAND CONTINGENT. During the Second World War Auster Rowe (far right) and mates from Truro had to learn the rudiments of skiing, while stationed in Iceland with their regiment.

ROYAL ENGINEERS' REUNION, c. 1960. All volunteers, these men served in Iceland, Italy and North Africa with the Cornish Regiment of the Royal Engineers. They are seen attending their annual dinner in the Royal British Legion Club (which used to be the old Grammar School) and part of the large wall-mounted arms of the city can be seen behind them. In the back row are: Lew Piper, Fred Andrews and Eric Allen. Also shown are Auster Rowe, Major Miles and Commanding Officer James Clift.

BOTTLE OF BUBBLY. This old stone bottle contained just what everybody needed for a celebration – locally brewed ginger beer. The bottle is in the possession of a local collector.

DUNKIRK VETERANS, *c*. 1960. Arthur Bunn, Charlie Savage and Bert Savage are the Cornwall contingent of the Dunkirk Veterans and are in Belgium for a reunion.

CORONATION, 1911. Boscawen Street was decked out with flowers and bunting for the Coronation of King George V. Most people seem to be wearing their Sunday best and the street is packed.

N. GILL AND HUGH RICE, 1911. Two of the most popular shops in Truro are shown beautifully decorated for the coronation of George V and Queen Mary. It seems to be early in the day as not many people are out and about and the milk is being delivered.

THE GREEN, *c*. 1880. A circus elephant has arrived at The Green pulling a heavily laden cart. In the background is the Customs House with its badge of the royal coat of arms over the door. Notice that there is no cathedral beyond the Customs House, confirming the early date of this photograph.

BACK QUAY. Jumbo (or Nellie) has arrived at Back Quay between Gills and the Municipal Buildings and leads the parade alongside the river approaching Lemon Bridge.

HEAVY SNOWFALL, *c.* 1900. St George's Road is blanketed with a layer of snow as we look down towards Ferris Town past the church of St George the Martyr and St George's chapel. Brunel's wooden viaduct is stark against the grey sky.

FLOODS, 1988. Sudden floods in 1988 caught many people unawares and unfortunately it was not for the first time. The police and fire brigade have launched their trusty vessel and mount a rescue bid in St Nicholas Street.

TEA TREAT, 1911. This is the first tea treat at Tresillian. It was held at the rectory and is believed to show Revd Watkins in charge.

FEOCK REGATTA, c. 1950. Feock Regatta was a very popular occasion and Loe Beach was always crowded. This is the starting boat with Michael Marshall on the left, Mr Stoot on the right and Nigel Ferris beside him, drinking from a pop bottle.

CHRISTMAS PARTY, late 1940s. Residents of the Kea/Playing Place/Carnon Downs area celebrate Christmas in some style. Nellie Davey, holding her son Geoffrey, is at the top right of the picture with Mrs Frost below her. Mrs Greet is to the left of Father Christmas with Joan Vincent beside her. John Pascoe is in the front, second from the left. Father Christmas was played by Cyril Holmes.

CELEBRATION AT CARVETH'S, *c.* 1960. The staff of Carveths raise their glasses but we are not sure what the occasion was. On the right is Alan Carveth and also in the group are Albert Trudgen, Clifton Ibbotson and George Singleton.

VJ DAY PARTY, 31 August 1945. The residents of Newham hold a street party to celebrate victory over Japan. At the head of the table, facing the camera, is Granny Webb. In the centre, in the white blouse, is Pat Marshall. At the far end is Rose Butcher. Third on the left is Mrs Chappell, fifth on left Mrs Penrose. Also in the photograph are Barbara and John Colston and Brian and Bernard Johns.

STREET PARTY, 1981. To celebrate the wedding of Prince Charles and Lady Diana Spencer a party was held in Kestle Drive, Highertown. Present are Byryn and Margaret Mitchell, Hedley and Rovena Brown, Gwen Andrews with Lydia Boyns and the rest of the Boyns family, Mr and Mrs Leverton, John Pascoe and his daughter, Helen, Lynne Golding and her son Simon, Ann Tregear and Mr Bennetts (in wheelchair).

ST GEORGE'S HALL, *c.* 1952. Mabel Lanxon holds a large cake bedecked with candles and bearing a model of the church. In the crowd are: top left, Diane Whitburn and in front of her, wearing a scarf, Gillian Barberry. To her right is Margaret Bennet and Steven Tyack. Also in the picture is Joyce Johns and down in the front, wearing a coat with a velvet collar, is Catherine Wingham.

WESLYAN PICNIC, 1908. Happy picnickers set off from Worth's Quay, watched by a miller in Trounson's corn mill on Trafalgar Wharf.

NEW CATHOLIC CHURCH, *c.* 1971. Trafalgar roundabout appears deserted and very bare, the large trees of today are small saplings in this view. The smart new Roman Catholic church under construction replaced the old building in Chapel Hill.

CHRISTMAS PARTY, *c.* 1963. This party was held in the City Hall by the Western National Bus Company. In amongst the crowd are Helen and Linda Westcott, Monica Penhaligon, Linda Wyatt and Sheryl Thomas.

TRURO CARNIVAL, *c.* 1948. A happy Patricia Carveth has won first prize with her beautifully decorated bicycle depicting a chicken made mostly, apparently, from hydrangeas. Her father was a horticulturalist who had decorated many carnival floats in his time.

TRURO CARNIVAL, *c.* 1950. Young David Trudgen displays his brightly decorated tricycle in Hendra playing field while waiting to join the carnival procession.

Six

Getting About

For many years getting from A to B for most ordinary Trurorians meant walking. Some rather more fortunate souls ran to the luxury of a bicycle but with Truro's steep hills much time was spent pushing the bike and walking. Those who could afford it had horse-drawn transport until motor cars arrived on the scene. Here we see a selection of various forms of transport for travel by water, road and rail.

LEMON BRIDGE, c. 1920. This large old lorry trundles along Back Quay, opposite the motor works and petrol pumps on Lemon Quay, which shows that motorized transport was now becoming more common. The large building on Lemon Quay is the Great Western Furniture warehouse and the premises of E.D. Lean, cycle and motor engineer, is next door.

BACK QUAY AND LEMON BRIDGE, *c.* 1920. Granite setts pave the foreground in Lemon Street as we look down Back Quay. The coalman appears to have parked his horse and cart outside the Municipal Buildings under a sign which reads 'Fire Engine', so hopefully there were no emergencies that morning! Beyond Taylor's garage is the old gasworks.

LEMON QUAY CAR PARK, *c.* 1964. Since the covering over of the river about thirty years ago this has been a carpark. There is a good selection of cars of the time in view. The attendant's hut is towards the right of the picture and 'Pay and Display' hasn't yet been thought of!

TRAFALGAR GARAGE, c. 1965. This was a Shell garage situated at the end of St Austell Street, opposite the police station. The row of cottages on the left led towards Boscawen Bridge and included a very popular fish and chip shop.

HICKS' SHOWROOM, 1966. An elegant Triumph GT6 sports car sits in the window of the Hicks showroom in City Road. We are looking up Infirmary Hill with the Tax Offices on the left, the staff keeping their beady eyes on those who could afford to buy elegant sports cars. On the left of the picture can be seen the top of the roof of a chapel which has since been demolished.

HICKS AND SON, *c.* 1918. This is the other side of the premises shown earlier (p. 58) and faces onto Kenwyn Street (No. 114). This marvellous old vehicle has travelled a long way – its number plate shows that it was registered in Kirkudbright, Scotland.

A 1947 STANDARD EIGHT, early 1950s. Albert (Abbey) Trudgen looks delighted with his car.

A 1937 MORRIS 8. Harry Andrews gazes fondly at his pride and joy. He had owned it for many years because it was necessary for him to use a car when he went to inspect work performed by Post Office telephones engineers.

BOSCAWEN STREET, c. 1967. This photograph was taken just one month before the demolition of the Red Lion. Little has changed in Boscawen Street except the appearance of the vehicles. A ten year old Daimler drives majestically towards us and a Rover taxi sits in the rank beside the war memorial.

ST ERME CHURCH, *c.* 1904. A pony and carriage waits outside St Erme church in about 1904. This is a peaceful scene at a time when other activities in Truro were hectic – the cathedral and the new viaduct were both under construction. This postcard was sent to a Miss Pedlar of Lanivet and all that was written on it was, 'Hope you will have a good collection', suggesting that everybody in Miss Pedlar's circle of friends was sending her cards.

THAT THING, *c.* 1950. This 1946 registered Commer pick-up was the vehicle to which Mrs Peggy Pollard entrusted her harp when travelling to perform at bardic ceremonies. Before being locally registered it had been a military vehicle and was in a 'bit of a state'. In this picture it is parked in Pydar Street (see p. 28).

CHIVERTON GARAGE, *c.* 1924. Five motorcyclists are gathered on the forecourt of Wards Garage at Chiverton. The assortment of headgear shows more elegance than safety consciousness and the lady pillion passenger on the right is wearing a cloche hat. Today Chiverton Garage has moved to the opposite side of the road but the bungalow is still there.

PLAYING PLACE GARAGE, *c.* 1936. This is Archie Tallack's garage at Playing Place. Left to right are: Mr Deeble and his grandson (?), Archie Tallack, Willie (Titch) Westcott and Bill Haswell.

WATERFALL GARDENS, *c.* 1900. A steam train leaves Truro railway station and crosses Brunel's viaduct on the main line to St Austell over the peaceful gardens beside St Georges church.

LEAVING TRURO BY RAIL, *c.* 1910. Just a decade after the previous picture, this train is travelling over the new viaduct, also heading for St Austell. The little boy with the dog watches the train but the little girl in her snowy-white pinafore is more interested in the camera.

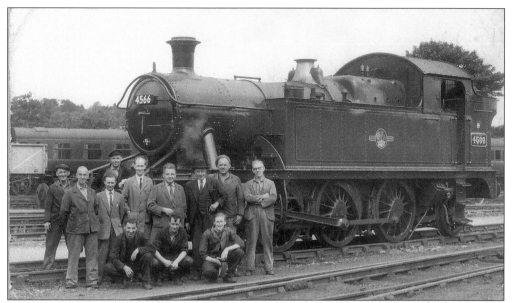

LAST STEAM TRAIN, 1959. This is the last steam engine, splendidly reconditioned and refurbished, to run prior to the introduction of the diesels. Photographed at Truro railway station, the men are, back row: Gordon Reddaway (driver). Left to right, second row: Alf Dart, Dick Lord, Phil Matthews, Derick Collins, Chris Combes, Joe Stephens (in the bowler hat, local shed master), Tommy Smale and Clifford Webb. Seated: Garfield Bellamy, Kit Cummins and an unidentified apprentice. The train is still in use today, on the Paignton to Kingswear line.

PENWEATHERS, c. 1900. A steam train crosses the viaduct at Penweathers. The date is uncertain but it is possible that this and all the other photographs of Brunel's viaducts used in this book (they come form the same source) could be from a time as early as the 1880s.

SHEPHERDS, *c.* 1930. This little station was on the St Newlyn East branchline and was apparently well used in the 1930s. The lady in the forground is Lottie Claxton.

70019 'LIGHTNING', 1948. *Lightning* enters Truro and is about to go under Black Bridge in 1948, the first engine to do so after the nationalisation of British Rail.

70019 'LIGHTNING', 1995. On 21
October 1995 the same engine (opposite)
steamed through Truro again, much to
the delight of railway enthusiasts.

DERAILMENT, 1951. On 22 May 1951 a goods train was derailed at Penweathers junction.
A worse disaster was averted when the 'up express' was halted just in time to avoid running
into it.

CHEVROLET CHARABANC, 1924. Albert Colston is the driver of the charabanc and Mr and Mrs Chinnery Richards of Kenwyn Mews garage stand by. The vehicle has 'Unity Tours' printed on the side and is parked in Kenwyn Street outside Tonkin's Vinegar Ope.

W.H. COLLINS AND SON, c. 1987. By 1987 the Vinegar works had disappeared although the ope still went through to Ferris Town and Collins' Garage occupied quite a large site. Today Collins' has also gone and part of the site is a temporary car park.

WEDDING DAY, *c.* 1930. Alfred Richards (left) and Albert Colston wait for the bride to emerge from a house in Daniell Road.

SOLEMN OCCASION, *c.* 1930. Albert Colston and two colleagues stand beside a Model T Ford hearse. It was the first motorized hearse in Truro and was owned by Chinnery Richards of Kenwyn Mews Garage.

STREETS OF LADOCK, *c.* 1965. The country buses were a familiar sight in the town and parked here on The Green is one of the 'Ideal Coaches' from Ladock. A lorry belonging to Percy Seacombe, Potato Merchant, is parked beside the river.

FAMILY DAY OUT, *c.* 1930. Chinnery Richards and family are driven on a day out by Albert Colston.

CASTLE STREET, 1946. The children have come out to see Harry Westcott sitting on the bonnet of a 1938 Austin 10 Glamorgan. It was used as a taxi, was owned by Harold Brown and driven by Harry.

TAXI RANK, *c. 1936.* Drivers Albert Colston and colleague both have Austins to drive. The newer one on the right was registered in 1936 but the other is considerably older. The rank occupies the same place today although the Hotel Central has disappeared.

KING HARRY FERRY. The ferry company was founded in 1888 and is still going strong today. This postcard was posted in 1905 and shows one of the earlier ferries.

KING HARRY FERRY, 1957. By 1957 the ferry was a little more sophisticated and designed for carrying motor cars rather than horse-drawn vehicles. By today's standards, though, it still looks pretty old-fashioned.

HIGH TIDE AT TRURO, c. 1975. Two little cabin cruisers sit below the car park opposite the warehouses in Malpas Road and there is what looks like a dredger moored up to the quayside.

MORRIS 8, AGAIN! Harry Andrews just couldn't resist taking just one more picture of his little car before putting it away in the garage for the night.

BOSCAWEN BRIDGE, *c.* 1955. A yacht graces the river below Boscawen Bridge.

Seven

The Best Days
of Our Lives?

For many people schooldays are looked back on as the best days of their lives but others look back in horror at those formative years. Whichever category people belong to, they still enjoy looking at old school photographs and trying to put names to the faces of their erstwhile friends or fellow sufferers. Of the schools shown in this chapter I believe that Bosvigo is the only one which still exists.

CLASS OF BOYS, c. 1930. This was either Truro Tech' or the top class at Daniell Road when they had boys, preparatory to secondary school. Left to right, back row: Dick Steer, Hilmer Brannlund, Tredger, B. Kent, Hoskins, Doble, Howard Granville, Walters, Rex Jennings, Endean, D. Sly, Pearse. Middle row: J. Walk, R. Gay, Hanum, Dyer, Wills, Marshall, Randall, Bell, Behenna, Penrose, Blee, Salmon, Pound, Seymour, Bartel. Front row: Behenna, Carter, Trudgeon, Rees, Robins, Jones, Cockle, Edwards, Nicholls, Hamilton, Miller, Jose.

CHYVELAH SCHOOL, *c.* 1940. This school no longer exists but was at Threemilestone. Here it is complete with its bell tower which was one of the first features to disappear over the years.

CHYVELAH, CLASS OF 1940. Among the children pictured are Chacewater boys, David May (extreme right, second row) and Bob Hop.

CHYVELAH, CLASS OF 1947. The teacher is Lottie Deeble. Jean Bastian is in the front row, second from left and included in those behind her are Rodney Billing, Marlene Wills, Paul Newton and David Hosking.

CHYVELAH SCHOOL. This is a later view of the school, without the bell tower, and not long before the the building was demolished.

ST GEORGE'S SCHOOL, *c.* 1925. These lovely striped ties were red and white and the cap badges bore the cross of St George. Left to right, back row: Ivor Gent, Arthur Crook, -?-, Ernie Colliver, Bernard Treloar, Horace Searle, Harry Bradley. Middle row: -?-, John Rapsey, ? McIntyre, Clifford Doole, Leslie Baker. Front row: Billy Chapple, Billy Stevens, Fred Mitchell, Harold Pascoe, Horace Leverton, ? Clemo, Abbey Trudgen.

TRURO SECONDARY MODERN BOYS' SCHOOL, *c.* 1946. This school was usually known as Truro Tech'. The boys are, left to right, back row: Raymond Kellow, Graeme Penhaligon, Michael Allen, Bill Ward, Bernard Kerslake, Douglas Colliver, Trevor Hawke, Vernon Parsons. Middle row: Stuart Gilbert, Trevor Powell, Derek Walker, Michael Keogh, David Cook, ? Peters, David May, -?-, Clive Duke, Mr Congdon. Front: Ernest Johns, ? Hughes, -?-, Gerald Allen, Leonard Hosking, Dennis Mitchell, ? Davies, -?-, Kingsley Ash.

HOMETOWN, 1962. Girls from Truro County Grammar School took part in Westward Television's *Hometown*, a local knowledge quiz game played between schools in the Westward TV area. The girls are, left to right: Christine Mitchell, Corrine Waters, Avril Hiley and Judith Solomon.

TRURO COUNTY SCHOOL, 1954. Left to right, back row : Carol Pascoe, Daphne Smitheram, Helen Patience, Pat Gallagher, Ann Trebilcock, -?-, Jane Hocking, Margaret Secreton, -?-, -?-, Leonie Spry, -?-, -?-. Middle row: Gloria Whitford, Patricia Parnell, -?-, Jacqueline Stone, -?-, Miss Bell, Pat Gay, Diane Bennetts, -?-, Jennifer Cokes, -?-. Front row: -?-, Beryl Hocking, Caroline Strutt, -?-, -?-, Teresa Gilbert, -?-, -?-, Angela Watts.

KEA SCHOOL, EARLY 1920s. Left to right, back row: Howard Mills, Garfield Dunstan, Clarence Scoble, Harold Harfoot, Edgar Davey, Reg Davey, Ted Keast, Freddie Behenna. Middle row: Aubrey Jose, Mona Lewarne, Lillian Jose, Maggie Golley, Gwen Burley, Phyllis Treganowan, Wilfred Gallihawke, Frankie Gunn, Stan Jose. Front row: Bill Deacon, Gracie Trebilcock, Eloise Dunstan, Gwen Dunstan, Alice Keast, Hazel Jose, Gracie Gunn, Ernie Cock, Garland Harfoot, Reg Behenna.

ST NEWLYN EAST CHURCH SCHOOL, 1931. Mr Teague, the headmaster, is shown with his pupils, who are: Eunice Mitchell, Gwen Stafford, May Grey, Joyce Harris, May Jennings, Grace Goodman, Edith Huthinance, Winifred Glanville, John Grant, Willie Goodman, Sam Hunkin, Ernest Philp, Norman Cross, Victor Tippet, William Glanville, John Waters, Andrew Jolly, Howard Tregunna, Sam Williams, Dorothy Waters, Megan Morcombe, Gwen Johnson, Madge Trethewey, Vera Carhart, Frank Mitchell, Tommy Stafford, Jack Moses, Sam Trethewey, Bradford Trethewey and William Harris.

FEOCK SCHOOL, c. 1945. Mrs Roseveare is seen here surrounded by her pupils, who included at this time some evacuees. Identified are: Tony Richards, Harold Ferris, Raymond Crocker, Johnny Blackburn, Brian Ferris, Heather Jay, Shirley Owen, Connie Roseveare, Ann Trebilcock, Ann Roseveare, Carol Westell, Marilyn Owen, John Roseveare and Lorna Rich.

ST PAULS SCHOOL, 1947. The teacher, Mrs Vincent, is on the extreme right beside George Cockle. Mary Stethridge is in the centre of the front row and also in the picture are: Wendy Clift, Ann Davey, Joan Clift, Dorothy Chappell, Barbara Hicks, Jean Curgenven, Brian Trewhella, Sylvia Trebell, Margaret Nancarrow and Diane Dawes.

ST MARYS INFANTS SCHOOL, 1925. This photograph was taken during Easter 1925 and the only person identified is Joyce Roberts, who is in the second row, third from the right.

ST MARYS SCHOOL. Here we have a glimpse of the former St Marys school, with the attractive garden beside it, which was tended by Truro City Council. Head gardener at the time was Mervyn Steeds. The top of the arched entrance from Pydar Street can be seen by the top of the bushes. This is where the Ministry of Agriculture's building now stands.

ST MARYS SCHOOL, *c.* 1948. Front row, fourth from left, is Joyce Gill and on the right hand end of the row is Gloria Andrew. Also on the front row, third from the right, is Ruth Haynes. In the middle row, third from the right is Brian Duke.

ST MARYS, 1955. Only four of these children can be identified at the time of writing and they are Angela Rapsey, Jane Andrews, Patricia Peartree and Margaret Dingle.

BOSVIGO SCHOOL, 1936. Left to right, back row: -?-, Peter Andrews, Derek Anstis, Ivor Dodd, ? Holland, Brian Knee(?), Roy Oates, ? Walters, ? Phillips, Miss Weekes. Middle row: Vera Jose, -?-, Vera Opie, Betty Rickard, Barbara Colston, Pamela Bellamy, Sheila Stevens. Third row: -?-, Velma Francis, Florence Blake, Joan Friend, Joan Harding, Ruth Arthur, Eileen Clemens, Mary Matthews. Front row: ? Beaumont, Bernard Seymour, Kenneth Venton, Billy Hawke, -?-.

BOSVIGO, 1939. This class included a number of evacuees from London and Plymouth but not all of the children can be identified: In the back row are: Kingsley Gummow, Ronnie Johns, June Venton, Pat Brannlund, Jean Richards. Middle row: Gloria Stone, Rosemary Hosking, Mary Barnes, Jean Venton. Front row: Michael Martin, Peter Eathorne, John Andrews, Dennis Solomon, Wilfred Phillips and George Champion.

BOSVIGO, 1949. Left to right, back row: Paul Edmonds, John Woodman, Violet Curnow, Anita Bertolucci, Alfreda Bosanko, Ann Braund, Dawn Pinfield, Janet Stoot, -?-, -?-. Second row: Pat Yeo, Madeleine Yeo, Robina Edgler, Pearl Williams, Loveday Piper, Brenda Pedley, Marion Satterley, Mary Ruse, Jennifer Tonkin, Jennifer Rule, Sheila Barnes. Third row: Brian Johns, Jonathan Warren, ? Rule, Terry Wyatt, Geoffrey Hicks, Peter Parnell, -?-, -?-, Peter Brown. Front row: George Lovering, Victor Cockle, -?-, Derek Chester, Brian Robinson, Preston Williams, -?-, Rex Lanfier.

BOSVIGO, 1950. Left to right, back row: Norman Croucher, John Harcourt, John House, Manny Cockle, Tommy Palmer, Bernard Johns, Peter Tippet, Brian Knott, David Fillbrook, Roger Webb, Derek Reynolds. Second row: Jackie Stone, Jean Penhaligon, Gillian Pawley, Maureen Pedley, Maureen Nicholls, Pat Gallagher, -?-, Christine Collins, Ann Pountney, Caroline Strutt, Diane Bennett. Third row: Heather Johns, -?-, Marion Hardy, Honor Davy, Janet Reed, Patricia Parnell, Pearl Sherman, Pat Gay, -?-, Pat Toy. Front row: Peter Bowden, Roger Yeo, Andrew Tresidder, John Moyse, Tony Wright, Peter Thomas, Robert Haslock and David James.

BOSVIGO, *c.* 1950s. Left to right, back row: Peter Wilson, Raymond Waite, Brian Hancock, Roger Bowden, Peter Reynolds, Terry Reynolds, Colin Clift, Kevin Murphy, Brian Lean, Tony Moxley. Second row. Philip Heayn, Richard Martin, Tanya(?) Rapsey, Pat Stone, -?-, Jennifer Colliver, Mary Trethewey, Ann Wilcox, -?-, Nigel Penelum, Richard Bowden. Third row: -?-, -?-, Margaret Williams, -?-, Angela Solomon, Margaret Augard, Margaret Skewes, -?-, Christine Eades, Sheila Richards, -?-. Front row: -?-, Dennis Stone, James Gummow, -?-, David Lobb, Edwin Bennett and Paul Bennett.

BOSVIGO, 1958. Left to right, back row: Carol Kinsman, Pamela Orton, Louise Amsdon, Valerie Fry, Sandra Luke, Sarabeth Waite, Rosalind Hooper, Angela Webb, Elizabeth Reed, Delma Notman, Colin Trudgeon. Second row: Susan Penhaligon, Eileen Venton, Dorothy Pope, Gwenda Lewis, Catherine Wingham, Patricia Venton, Elizabeth Annear, Margaret Marshall, Carol Mylan, Pauline Jeffery, Mary Lobb, Heather Bennett, Susan Hawkey, David Cavill. Third row: Christopher Farley, Geoffrey Johns, Keith Escott, John Green, -?-, John Best, Glenn Brown, Peter Wilton, Denis Heayn, Donald Medland, Richard Williams, Barry Williams. Front row: Michael Rule, Nigel Cox, -?-, Michael Grundy, Geoffrey Morris, Barry Thomas, Paul Wilkinson, Philip Cooper,-?-, Roger Ray.

BOSVIGO, c. 1962. The back row includes: Linda Westcott, Joanna Scott, Susan Steadman and Susan Palmer. The second row includes: Alan Bennett, Lesley Knight, Pauline Hill, Mary Hewings, Yvonne Curd and Pat Verran. Third row includes: Robert Hoskin, Malcolm Tucker, Tony Pearce, Graham Hill, Philip Lindford, Michael Richards and Steven Pentecost. The front row includes: Colin Hankin, Tony Ray, John Jose, Patrick Moon and Nigel Dickinson. The teacher is Mrs Green.

NOT QUITE SCHOOL AGE? Four young Mitchells line up on the pavement outside their house in the early 1920s. They are Arnold, Doris, Cedric and Douglas.

THE BIG FINISH, *c.* 1890. Never mind school, this is much more fun!